Utrecht
&
CHILDREN

Anika Redhed

Utrecht 2016

© Anika Redhed, 2016

Editor: Kate Wood
Cover photo: Harrison Redhed
Cover design: Musthafa

All rights reserved. This book or any portion thereof may not be reproduced or used in any manner whatsoever without the express written permission of the publisher except for the use of brief quotations in a book review. Behind The Sights, Utrecht, The Netherlands, info@behindthesights.one.

Table of contents

Introduction

Chapter 1

    Museums

Chapter 2

    Inside the moat

Chapter 3

    Playgrounds & Petting Zoos

Chapter 4

    Sports & Entertainment

Chapter 5

    Child Friendly Gastronomy

Chapter 6

    Shops

Chapter 7

    Miffy

Chapter 8

    Paper Chase Route

Chapter 9

    Practical Information

Introduction

Riding a fake train through virtual space or paddling through the water of the old canal, after reading this guide you will wish you were still a child. Don't worry: just take some children, either your own or borrowed, bring them to Utrecht and join them while they explore the town. A city trip can be just as much fun with the entire family as it is alone. This goes for every city, but especially for Utrecht, because the downtown area is one big playground for all ages.

You will have to take your pick from all the diversions that are on offer, depending on age and interests. In this guide are the main sights that can be of interest to children, as well as some entertainment that is specifically for them. Then there are some child friendly restaurants mentioned. Most restaurants will welcome you and anyone you bring along, but some have special kids' corners and menus.

The focus of this guide is on the downtown area, roughly everything that is within the moat. You could spend your entire day here, doing everything on foot without the hassle of public transportation or one way streets. In a special section of the book, the entertainment in the other areas of town is mentioned. At the end of the book, you can find a suggested walking tour combined with a paper chase and a few suggestions for small games to kill time or complete the fatigue on the way back to the hotel.

Dutch names are printed in *italic*. Opening hours are mentioned, but prices are not, since they are apt to frequent change. At the time of publication, the information in this guide was accurate, but things change fast. We try to update the guide as often as we can, but we cannot keep track of all changes. Please check websites, or ask at your hotel or the tourist information office. And follow us on Facebook: Secrets of Utrecht. We would be happy with any updates, questions and comments! Send us a message through Facebook.

1. Museums

The museums in Utrecht are very diverse and whether they are good for you depends on the age of your children and their personal interests. An overview video: http://bit.ly/1YbpNUj. A full list of all museums in Utrecht can be found here:
http://www.museautrecht.nl/en/info/fancy-a-day-trip.html (English)
http://www.museautrecht.nl/de/info/home.html (Deutsch)

Descriptions of what the museums have on offer for children:
http://www.museautrecht.nl/en/voor-kinderen.html (English)
http://www.museautrecht.nl/de/fur-kinder.html (Deutsch)

Most museums are closed on Mondays, except for Holidays. Never try to do anything on January 1st, April 27th and December 25th.

University Museum - *Universiteitsmuseum*
There are interactive displays between the elephant-nose fish skeletons and preserved fetuses. You can have your picture taken as if your own head was put into a jar filled with formaldehyde, but the real highlight is the youth lab. Every kid has his own working station with a folder filled with experiments. All the materials required are in the little drawers, or elsewhere in the room. You children can determine which tongue belongs to which animal, sit on a chair of nails, or create bubbles in water using a pencil and a battery. Best suited to kids between 6 and 12. The folders should be in Dutch and English and there is usually an assistant present who can help out with everything.
Address: Lange Nieuwstraat 106
Open: Every day (also Monday!): 10:00 – 17:00
Web: http://www.universiteitsmuseum.nl/english

Miffy Museum - *Nijntje Museum*
This is not so much a museum as it is an indoor Miffy playground. There are lots of hands on activities, puzzles, a kitchen, a shed with workmate, a slide, a traffic park with a little bicycle and everything is in Miffy style: bright colours and simple drawings. It is free for those under 2 years of age and everybody over 12 pays a reduced admission. It is mainly fun for those up to 6/7 years old. Books are read on Sunday afternoons and there

are creative workshops on weekends in the art room on the 1st floor.
Because of the crowds, the museum has started working with time frames. Within a certain frame a maximum number of tickets is sold. Once you are inside, you can stay as long as you like. During weekends and vacations it is best to reserve your tickets in advance. Tickets are sold in the Central Museum across the street. They also sell a collection of Miffy souvenirs.
Address: Agnietenstraat 2
Open: Tue – Sun: 10:00 – 17:00.
Web: http://nijntjemuseum.nl/?lang=en

Railway Museum - *Het Spoorwegmuseum*
The most expensive of all museums, but this is because it is an amusement park in disguise. A shaking elevator will not only take you down, but also 100 years back in time to the days when the first steam engine had just been made. You can board a train and get startled, because there is another locomotive about to frontally hit yours. If you survive, you can board another train and virtually ride through high, snowcapped mountains and space. At the end of the day you will be begging the museum guards to let you into the jumbo express running around the grounds, or the little boats going to and from the light house. They also have a lot of trains, small ones, railway signs and

real trains. Many of them have interactive displays inside. Fun for most ages, except maybe the very young.
Address: Maliebaanstation 16
Open: Tue – Sun: 10:00 – 17:00.
Web: http://www.spoorwegmuseum.nl/ (only Dutch)

Utrecht Archives - *Het Utrechts Archief*
This is way more fun than its name suggests. And it is free.
This is a small museum of the history of Utrecht. Some exhibits change twice a year, some are permanent. The building was once a monastery and the remains can be seen in the cellar, including a talking virtual monk. Many years later it was a courthouse and some of the old cells are being used

as displays. The highlight is the carriage in which you can take a ride. It is a bit shaky, but you get to see the town and surroundings as they were centuries ago. The coachman is a bit talkative, but since it is free at all times there is really no reason to complain.
Address: Hamburgerstraat 28
Open: Tue – Fri: 10:00 – 17:00, Sat & Sun: 12:30 – 17:00.
Web: http://www.hetutrechtsarchief.nl/english

Museum of self-playing musical instruments
– Museum Speelklok
Lots of music and mechanical instruments with moving parts. There is, for example, a music box with a bunny coming out of an egg. Kids can make their own music box or do a paper chase.
Address: Steenweg 6
Open: Tue – Sun: 10:00 – 17:00.
Web: https://www.museumspeelklok.nl/lang/en/

Grocery store museum - *Kruideniersmuseum Betje Boerhave*
This is a little candy shop from the 20th century which still looks that way. The merchandise is sold from glass pots and weighed with an old fashioned scale. The staff wear white aprons and put your candy in a paper cone. On the upper floor they have a bunch of grocery items from the last century. They

are very proud of their shop and are willing to let you try some old Dutch candy.
Address: Hoogt 6
Open: Tue – Sat: 12:30 – 16:30.
Web: http://www.kruideniersmuseum.nl/route (mainly Dutch)

Bastion and Astronomy – *Sonnenborgh Museum*
All about the sun and the stars. There is a paper chase and a route for toddlers from 3-6 years where they follow the footsteps of aliens. See what it is like to be a 16th century soldier and learn about meteorites, stars and planets. On Sundays you can stare at the sun.
Address: Zonnenburg 2
Open: Tue – Fri: 11:00 – 17:00, Sun: 13:00 – 17:00.
Web: http://www.sonnenborgh.nl/page=site.treenode/tree=english

DOMunder
This is partly fun because it is fairly dark underground and you walk around with the provided torch. But there are also lots of stones and rocks down there. Kids would need a special interest in archeology/history to enjoy this. Reservations are required during weekends and vacations.

Address: Domplein 4
Open: Tue – Sun: 10:30 – 16:30 (last entrance).
Web: http://www.domunder.com/en

Dom Tower – *Domtoren*
If your kids have too much energy, this might be the way to solve it. There are 465 steps to tackle. The stairways are very windy and tight. You get to see the giant bells and the view over the city is great. Best to reserve in advance.
Address: Domplein 21
Open: Sun, Mon: 12:00 – 17:00, Tue – Sat: 10:00 – 17:00.
Web: http://www.domtoren.nl/en

2. Inside the moat

When the weather permits, it is great fun to enjoy the town from the water side. When you follow the old or new canal, you have a great view of the city and the old wharves and facades. Underneath every lantern by the water is a corbel with a display. These refer to myths, religion, the name of the closest house or trades. You have a great view of them from the water.

Canal Bike
Water bicycles.
Address: Oudegracht close to #167
Open: Wed – Sun 10:00 – 18:00 (April, May, June, September, October), every day 10:00 – 18:00 (July & August).
Web: https://www.canal.nl/en/canal-bike-utrecht (English)
https://www.canal.nl/fr/canal-bike-utrecht (français)
https://www.canal.nl/de/canal-bike-utrecht (Deutsch)
https://www.canal.nl/it/canal-bike-utrecht (italiano)
https://www.canal.nl/es/canal-bike-utrecht (español)

Canoes are for rent as well. You can start downtown and paddle all the way out to the forest at *Rhijnauwen*, have a drink or something to eat and go back (about 5 kilometers one way). Or you can stay on the canals. You can book tours during day and night as well.

Kano Verhuur Utrecht
Canoes for rent. Only one-person canoes.
Address: Oudegracht 275
Open: 13:00 – 21:00, Tue – Sun 10:00 – 20:00. Between mid October and mid February only open for appointments.
Web: http://kanoverhuurutrecht.nl/ (only Dutch)

De Rijnstroom
Canoes for rent. Tours, also at night, or individual rent.
Address: Weg naar Rhijnauwen 2 (outside of the moat)
Open: Every day 09:30 – 18:00 (April & September), Every day 09:30 – 22:00 (May – August).
Web: http://www.rijnstroom.nl/ (only Dutch)

Library
In the central library downtown there is a kid's corner. Children between 3 and 7 can watch a digital picture book. Entrance is free and you can read books inside. There are many seats and tables and a small cafe. To borrow books you need to be a paid member.
Address: Oudegracht 167
Open: Mon 13:00 – 21:00, Tue, Wed, Fri 10:00 – 18:00, Thu 10:00 – 21:00, Sat 10:00 – 17:00, Sun 13:00 – 17:00.

Web: http://www.bibliotheekutrecht.nl/vestigingen/alle-vestigingen/openingstijden.264931.html (only Dutch)

Workshops

There are all kinds of workshops on offer. Most are cooking and creative stuff. If you are not a group, you have to go to one of the so-called walk ins (*inloop*). Reserving in advance is advisable. Below is one example. You can also google 'workshops Utrecht'.

Grachtenatelier
Address: Oudegracht 185 Wharf Side
Web: www.grachtenatelier.nl (only Dutch)
List for walk-ins:
http://www.grachtenatelier.nl/workshops/inloopagenda (only Dutch)

Playground The Little Dom – *Speeltuin De Kleine Dom*

Public playground up to 12 years. Climbing, soccer field, swings, sand & water, small pool when the weather is good, little bikes and trampolines. Indoor games, handicrafts, toys. Entrance is free. Drinks available at a small fee.

Address: Lange Nieuwstraat 79
Open: Mon – Fri 10:00 – 17:00, Sat & Sun 13:00 -17:00 (September – March), Mon – Fri 10:00 – 17:30 (April – August), Sat & Sun 13:00 – 17:00.
Web: http://www.doenjadienstverlening.nl/over-

doenja/locaties/de-kleine-dom/ (only Dutch)
There is a small outside playground with some playground equipment on the corner of *Nicolaasdwarsstraat* and *Wijde Doelen*.

Theatre *Toverknol*
Theatre for kids. They can dress up first. Clothes, lemonade and cookies are provided.
Address: Oudegracht 63
When: Wednesdays 10:30 (1-4 years), 14:00 (5-9 years)
Sat & Sun 10:30 (1-4 years), 12:15 (3-7 years), 14:00 (5-9 years)
Web: http://www.detoverknol.nl/index.php (only Dutch)

Wolff
Movie theatre showing mainstream movies.
Address: Radboudkwartier 19 (Hoog Catharijne), Jaarbeursplein 6 (Beatrixgebouw), Voorstraat 89
Web: http://www.wolff.nl/ (only Dutch)

Pathé Rembrandt
Movie theatre showing mainstream movies.
Address: Oudegracht 73
Web: https://www.pathe.nl/bioscoop/rembrandt (only Dutch)

TivoliVredenburg
This is a concert hall with all kinds of music and regular activities for children and families. Go to the

website and click on *familie* to get the schedule. One example is My First Festival: Music, musical theatre, baking your own pancakes, making your own movie. The first was held in May 2016, more dates are coming.
Address: Vredenburgkade 11
Web: https://www.tivolivredenburg.nl/nl/ (only Dutch)

3. Playgrounds & Petting Zoos

There are a few nice playgrounds around town, outside the moat:

Griftsteede
Petting zoo and playground. Every day at 15:30 they feed the animals. It is in a big, nice park directly north of the downtown area.
Address: Van Swindenstraat 129 (Griftpark)
Open: Tue – Fri 10:00 – 17:00, Sat & Sun 10:00 – 18:00.
Web: http://www.utrechtnatuurlijk.nl/locaties/griftsteede/ (only Dutch)

Torteltuin
This is in the same Griftpark, but for kids up to 7.
€ 1.00 per person
Address: Kwartelstraat 68
Open: Mon - Fri 09:30 – 17:30, Sat 11:30 – 15:30. Closed in January.
Web: http://www.torteltuin.nl/ (only Dutch)

Fort Luna
A bit out of the way, but a green outdoor playground with building materials, climbing, sand, water. They'll get dirty. Extra activities in vacations.

Address: Oude Liesbosweg 40
Open: Mon, Wed, Thu, Fri 12:00 – 17:30, Sat 10:00 – 17:00, Sun 13:00 – 17:00.
Web: http://www.lunetten.nl/fortluna/ (only Dutch)

Speelbos Gagelbos

Playing forest. Large field with climbing device, forest, ditch, rope bridge, funicular, flying fox. Hiking possibilities.
Address: Gageldijk (close to #104)
Open: Freely accessible.
Web: http://www.staatsbosbeheer.nl/natuurgebieden/groene-hart-vechtstreek/bezienswaardigheden/speelbos-gagelbos (only Dutch)

Speeltuin Eilandsteede

Playground situated in a park. Climbing and other equipment and petting farm.
Address: Vreugdenhillaan 31
Open: Tue – Sun 10:00 – 17:00. In summer vacation also on Mondays.
Web: http://www.doenjadienstverlening.nl/over-doenja/locaties/speeltuin-eilandsteede/ (Dutch only)

Nieuw Rotsoord

Petting zoo a little south of downtown.
Address: Briljantlaan 101
Open: Mon – Fri 11:00 – 17:00, Sat & Sun 13:00 – 17:00.
Web: http://www.nieuwrotsoord.nl/ (only Dutch)

Zaagmolen De Ster

A still-functioning saw mill. It is outside the moat (a ten minute walk from the central station) and they only open on Saturdays, but it is fun and interesting to see. Free tours also come in English and also cater to children. There is a very small petting zoo outside.

Video: http://bit.ly/1WOq4xq.
Address: Molenpark 3
Open: Saturday 13:00 – 16:00.
Web: http://www.molendester.nu/zaagdemonstraties-en-rondleidingen/ (only Dutch)

4. Sports & Entertainment

Possibilities for skating, swimming, bowling and large indoor playgrounds.

Farmer's Golf
In Dutch called *boerengolf*. There is a clog on a stick and with this you have to hit the ball into the dug holes in a pasture. There is a 'track' close to Utrecht in the town of Bunnik, so you could combine it with a visit to the Rhijnauwen forest. You have to be with a party of at least 6. Only with reservation.
Organized by: Restaurant Vroeg
Address: Achterdijk 1, Bunnik
Web: http://www.vroeg.nl/arrangementen/groepen-2/ (only Dutch)

Skate Parade
For larger kids there is a skate parade every Friday night in the summer months. About 25 kilometers / 15.5 miles, but speed is low.
Starting point: Lucasbolwerk
When: 20:00 – 22:15. Beginning of May until the end of September.
Web: http://u-skateparade.nl/ (only Dutch)

Vechtse Banen
Indoor ice-skating. Mainly in winter (September until March). Between April and September there is a thing called 'sommer ice' and there are possibilities on weekends: 12.00 - 13.30 and 13.30 – 15.00. Reservation is required. If you are interested in this, you had better send them an email first: administratie@vechtsebanen.nl
Address: Mississippidreef 151
Web: http://www.vechtsebanen.nl/p/18/83/-/2/schaatsen (only Dutch)

Skatepark Utrecht
For skateboarders.
Address: Koningin Wilhelminalaan 4
Open: Tue & Thu 15:00 - 22:00, Wed 14:00 – 22:00, Fri 15:00 – 24:00, Sat 13:30 – 22:00, Sun 13:30 – 21:00
Web: http://www.skateparkutrecht.nl/ (only Dutch)

Kids City
Indoor kids' heaven. Slides, trains, merry-go-rounds, etc.
Address: Vlampijpstraat 79
Open: Tue & Thu 10:00 – 19:00, Wed & Fri & Sat & Sun 10:00 – 18:00,
Web: http://kidzcity.nl/ (only Dutch)

Ballorig
Giant indoor playground with trampolines. Parents don't pay.
Address: Mississippidreef 22
Open: Mon - Fri 09:00 – 18:00, Sat & Sun 10:00 – 19:00.
Web: http://www.ballorig.nl/utrecht (only Dutch)

Bison Bowling
Bowling.
Address: Mariaplaats 13 A
Open: Mon 16:00 – 24:00, Tue & Wed & Thu 14:00 – 24:00, Fri & Sat 14:00 – 02:00, Sun 14:00 – 23:00.
Web: http://www.bisonbowlingutrecht.nl/ (only Dutch)

Gamestate
Largest game center in the country, including 4D-games and simulators.
Address: Mariaplaats 13
Open: Mon – Thu & Sun 12:00 – 24:00, Fri & Sat 12:00 – 01:00.
Web: http://www.gamestate.nl/

Laser Games Utrecht
Laser games.
Address: Biltstraat 4
Open: Wed 13:00 – 23:00, Thu 15:00 – 23:00, Fri 15:00 – 24:00, Sat 12:00 – 01:00, Sun 12:00 – 19:00.
Web: http://lasergamesutrecht.nl/ (only Dutch)

Kartfabrique
Karting, laser gaming and prison island (kind of an escape room, but with several rooms and also physical challenges).
Address: Westkanaaldijk 7
Open: Tue & Thu 16:00 – 23:00, Wed 13:00 – 23:00, Fri 16:00 – 24:00, Sat 10:00 – 24:00, Sun 13:00 – 22:00.
Web: http://www.kartfabrique.nl/kartbaan-utrecht/ (only Dutch)

Awesome space
Retro Computer games.
Address: Marco Pololaan 8-10
Open: Every Wed & Fri 19:00 – 23:00.
Web: https://awesomespace.nl/

Swimming pools
There are several swimming pools in town, but they are managed by the city. The question is not how to find them, but how to find out when they are open. You might want to ask your host or the tourist information office first. Anybody over 12 needs to show ID.

Den Hommel
Nice pool with several facilities. 'Family swimming' is meant for adults with kids. No more than 2 kids per adult. This swimming pool closes during the

entire summer vacation!
Address: Kennedylaan 5
Open: Family swimming on Friday 11:30 - 21:00 (the disco lights are turned on at 18:00). Also on Sat 11:00 – 14:00 and Sun 09:00 – 16:30. Except in summer vacation.
Web: https://www.utrecht.nl/wonen-en-leven/vrije-tijd/zwembaden/zwembad-den-hommel/rooster-en-openingstijden/ (only Dutch)

De Kwakel
Smaller and open in summer only, roughly in July and August.
Address: Paranadreef 10
Open: Family swimming Sat 12:00 – 17:00 every day and Sundays 09:00 – 16:00. It is open to everyone Mon, Wed, Fri 13:00 – 18:00.
Web: https://www.utrecht.nl/wonen-en-leven/vrije-tijd/zwembaden/zwembad-de-kwakel/rooster-en-openingstijden/ (only Dutch & complicated)

De Krommerijn
Only one regular swimming pool. When the weather is good, the roof opens. You need a monthly pass.
Address: Weg naar Rhijnauwen 3
Open: Every day 10:00 – 18:00 in July and August. For other months check the website.
Web: http://www.zwembaddekrommerijn.nl/swimming-in-the-most-beautiful-pool-of-utrecht/

Maarsseveense plassen
A lake in the north of town. Entrance fee required between € 3.00 and € 5.00 (2017).
Address: Herenweg 53
Open: Mid April to mid September every day 09:00 – 18:00.

Web: http://www.recreatiemiddennederland.nl/pagina/35/Maarsseveense_plassen.html (only Dutch)

Down Under
It is a large pond used for swimming, water-skiing, tubing, body-boarding (with disco version), wave surfing (indoor), wake-boarding and knee-boarding. It is not officially in Utrecht, but close enough. They also have an obstacle run, foot golf, beach and a restaurant. Entrance fee € 4 (2016).
Address: Ravensewetering 1, Nieuwegein
Web: http://www.downunder.nl/ (only Dutch)

5. Child Friendly Gastronomy

Most places will welcome you with children, but some places are better adjusted to them. This will give you more time to enjoy the breaks as well.

Yoghurt Barn
Yogurt in any combination, pastries, coffee and frozen yogurt. Special prices and quantities for kids under 6. Kids' corner.
Address: Vinkenburgstraat 15
Open: Mon – Wed 08:30 – 18:00, Thu 08:30 – 21:00, Fri & Sat 08:30 – 19:00, Sun 09:30 – 19:00.
Web: https://yoghurtbarn.nl/ (only Dutch)

Florin
Free kids' club every Sunday afternoon in the winter season. Kids are entertained on the upper floor and parents can have a drink or bite to eat down stairs.
Address: Nobelstraat 2
When: Every Sunday afternoon 14:00 – 17:30 (October until the end of March).
Web: http://www.florinutrecht.nl/ (partially English, partially Dutch)

De Rechtbank ('The Court')
There is a wonderful outside terrace with lounge

furniture. There are usually some toys for the kids and the terrace is separated from the road by a fence. Every Sunday 13:00 – 19:00 the place is turned into a kids' paradise, inside or outside depending on the weather.
Address: Korte Nieuwstraat 14
Open: Mon – Fri 06:30 – 24:00, Sat & Sun 07:30 – 01:00.
Web: http://derechtbank.com/ (only Dutch)

Stael
Kids' corner.
Address: Twijnstraat 9
Open: Every day 08:00 – 19:00.
Web: http://www.stael.nl/ (only Dutch)

Pannenkoekenbakkerij De Muntkelder
Pancakes are always a treat for kids. This one is by the water side in a wharf cellar.
Address: Oudegracht 112
Open: Mon – Sun 12:00 -21:00.
Web: http://www.deoudemuntkelder.nl/en/

Zussen ('Sisters')
They have a separate children's menu. The kids' corner is open every day 12:00 – 20:00. There is a pinball, TV and more. There is no adult supervision.
Address: Korte Jansstraat 23
Open: Mon & Tue 16:00 – 24:00, Wed 11:00 – 24:00, Thu 11:00 – 01:30, Fri 11:00 – 02:30, Sat 11:00 – 02:30,

Sun 12:00 – 24:00.
Web: http://www.zussen.com/ (only Dutch)

Café Centraal ('Cafe Central')

Their terrace is on the museum grounds and thus green, quiet and far from any traffic. There is a Miffy statue on the grass. They serve Miffy pastry and Miffy sandwiches.

Address: Agnietenstraat 1 (entrance is in the corner, behind the parking lot)
Open: Tue – Sun 10:00 – 18:00.
Web: http://centraalmuseum.nl/bezoeken/Horeca/
(Only Dutch. There is a page about the cafe in English, but it is not correct.)

Buurten (outside the moat)

There is room to change diapers in the bathroom. There is a special kids' corner with toys and they serve peanut butter sandwiches.

Address: Burgemeester Reigerstraat 61
Open: Every day at 09:00, Sun 10:00.
Web: http://www.kombuurten.nl/buurten-in-oost/ (only Dutch)

Vandaag ('Today')

Buffet style restaurant with a separate buffet for children. You don't pay for what you eat or drink, you pay for the time you spend inside. You have to choose between 2 or 3 hours in advance. It is out of the way, but it is nice for kids and there is free

parking. Only dinner and only with reservation.
Address: Proostwetering 80-L (outside the moat)
Open: Mon – Thu 17:00 – 22:00, Fri – Sun 16:30 – 22:00.
Web: http://www.restaurantvandaag.nl/en/vandaag-utrecht-2/

Eye Hotel
A hotel with two special family rooms.
Address: Wijde Begijnestraat 1-3
Web: http://www.eyehotel.nl/en

6. Shops

A few shops downtown that might be fun for parents who like to shop for their children. Or that like to play themselves.

The Joker – games store
Large supply of new and second hand games and a passion for playing. There are games played every Saturday night, and anyone can join. On Thursday and Friday, they play Magic Draft.
Address: Oudegracht 230A
Open: Mon, Tue, Wed 10:00 – 18:00, Thu, Fri, Sat 10:00 – the end of the game.
Web: http://www.the-joker.nl/ (only Dutch)

Subcultures – games store
Address: Oudegracht 183
Open: Mon 13:00 – 18:00, Tue, Wed 11:00 – 18:00, Thu & Fri 11:00 – 19:00, Sat 10:00 – 18:00, Sun 12:00 – 18:00.
Web: http://www.subcultures.nl/ (only Dutch)

Princes en Erwtje – clothes
Shoes, clothes (only baby's) and accessories.
Address: Oudegracht 220
Open: Tue - Thu 10:00 – 18:00, Sat 10:00 – 17:00, Sun

13:00 – 17:00.
Web: http://prinsesenerwtje.nl/ (only Dutch)

Babalade - furniture
Special and creative furniture & small stuff. The cellar goes all the way under the street to the wharf.
Address: Oudegracht 223
Open: Mon – Fri 10:00 – 18:00, Sat 10:00 – 17:00.
Web: http://www.babalade.nl/ (only Dutch)

Noahs – children's fashion
Your kid will be more fashionable than the average fashion blogger. Their website lets you look inside.
Address: Lijnmarkt 45
Open: Tue – Fri 10:00 – 18:00, Sat 10:00 – 17:00, Sun 13:00 – 17:00.
Web: http://www.noahs.nl/ (only Dutch)

Kakelbont – children's books
Also games, puzzles and toys.
Address: Oudegracht 200a
Open: Mon 13:00 – 18:00, Tue & Wed & Fri 10:00 – 18:00, Thu 10:00 – 19:00, Sat 10:00 – 17:30.
Web: http://nieuw.kakelbont.info/ (only Dutch)

De Utrechtse Kinderboekhandel – children's books
Also games, posters and stuffed animals from story books.
Address: Ganzenmarkt 10

Open: Mon 13:00 – 18:00, Tue, Wed, Fri 09:00 – 18:00, Thu 09:00 – 21:00, Sat 09:00 – 17:30, Sun 13:00 – 17:00.
Web: http://www.kinderboekwinkel.net/index.php?option=news&newsid=1&linkid=11 (only Dutch)

Kinderwinkel Westerkade – kids' everything
Clothes, gifts, decoration, art. Just outside the moat.
Address: Westerkade 19
Open: Tue – Sat 10:00 – 18:00, Sun 13:00 – 17:00.
Web: http://www.kinderwinkelwesterkade.nl/ (only Dutch)

7. Miffy

Large ears, a crossed mouth and a colourful dress: Miffy is one of the most famous does in the world. *Dick Bruna*, the father of Miffy, was born in 1927 in Utrecht. He was supposed to be a publisher just like his dad and grandfather, but he turned out to be more interested in arts. Eventually he became a drawer at the publisher. In 1955 Dick vacationed with his family at the seaside and told stories to his son. One day he saw a rabbit outside the window and based a story on the animal. His son liked those stories and Dick decided to draw it. Miffy was born. The books have been translated into more than 50 languages. In The Netherlands it is mainly a children's story and not something even 7-year olds can relate to. In Japan and some other parts of Asia, Miffy is popular with adults as well.

In Dutch the cute doe is called *Nijntje*, but she is also called Miffy, Miffi of Mifi.

In French : Mouffe or Petit Lapin

In German : Nientje or Ninchen

In Finnish : Milla

In Swedish : Lilla Kanin

The museum shop in the Central Museum has a range of Miffy souvenirs. Their cafe (no entrance ticket needed) offers Miffy pastries and Miffy sandwiches. They can even be served with the typical Dutch chocolate sprinkles (*hagelslag*).

There is a Miffy statue in the garden of the Central Museum and one right outside the Miffy Museum. A flat bronze one stands on the Miffy Square (*Nijntje Pleintje*). It is at the end of the Old Canal next to the *1e Achterstraat*.

At the edge of *Vredenburg* Square on the corner with the *Lange Viestraat* is a traffic light that doesn't have the standard figure, but a red and green Miffy. It is accompanied by a rainbow zebra.

Several bakeries in town sell chocolate Miffys:

Bakkerij Theo Blom
Also Miffy cookies and chocolates with the Dom Tower image.
Address: Zadelstraat 23
Open: Mon & Sat: 08:00 – 17:00, Tue – Fri: 08:00 – 18:00.
Web: http://www.banketbakkerijtheoblom.nl/view.asp?page=producten (only Dutch)

Sector 3
The neighbour of the kid-friendly Stael lunchroom sells large chocolate Miffys. Also colourful macarons

in 20 different flavours, as well as bread and chocolates. To sit or to go.
Address: Twijnstraat 7
Open: Every day 08:00 – 18:00.
Web: http://www.sector-3.nl/ (only Dutch)

For videos about Miffy and Utrecht:
http://bit.ly/1Tla2XJ

8. Paper Chase Route

Tea pots glued against tree trunks, lions and drunk deer: they can all be spotted downtown. Many locals don't even know to find these, so pretend you are a detective and become an expert on the downtown area of Utrecht and its many details.

This is a suggested route through a part of downtown. The description starts at Dom Square, but you can start anywhere on the route. If you want to visit some of the mentioned museums or playgrounds, you would have to be aware of the opening hours. You can keep your kids and yourself entertained by trying to find the animals and decorations mentioned below. The route is described. The 'treasures' are <u>underscored</u>, followed by a description of where to find them. Places of interest are printed **bold**.

Dom Square
Should you need any information or want to make any reservations, the tourist office is on the north side of the square. Take your kids shortly into the *Pandhof*, the little garden beside the Dom Church. You can enter it south of the church, close to the

large runic stone.

If you want to keep the children busy for a long time, let them search for the stone rope. This might take a while. It is in the first window you see when you enter the garden from the square, seemingly holding pieces of decoration together.

Start the walk in a southern direction into the *Lange Nieuwstraat*.

2 gold lions (left side #6 and #8)
It is the weapon of The Netherlands and also has a golden crown. This sign means this company is a 'purveyor to the court'. These days it is more of an honorary title, it doesn't mean this company actually delivers goods to the king.

Archives and restaurant *De Rechtbank* (left #14)

Golden sword (Above the entrance to the archives in the courtyard.)

Swan or goose (In the facade on the corner right with *Hamburgerstraat*.)

Bull's head (Left #34)

Lion's or bear's head (Right #43)

3 Deer (On the sign #47)
It is a shield with the name of the cafe. It is named after a hostelry from around the 17th century.

Cow's leg and hoof (Between #61 and #63)

Playground *De Kleine Dom*. (#77)

Turn left into the *ABC straat*, named this because there was once a school in here where kids learned the alphabet.

2 Hands (left #32)

Turn right at the end of the street. On the corner is bakery *Moolenbeek* which has been there since 1873. You could have a cookie or sandwich to go. Walk past the New Canal (*Nieuwegracht*). It was dug at the end of the 14th century. So pretty old, for something called 'new'. At the time it was compared with the other canal that had been there for a few hundred years, so this one was the new one.

Bell (left road side #163)
In the old days whenever there was a house on fire, people would ring this bell. There were also times when every house by law had to have a certain amount of buckets. When there was a fire, people would form a chain between the canal and the

house, passing buckets along.

<u>Beer barrel</u> (#197)
<u>Dog</u> (on the pavement in the park near the bridge)
There once lived an artist nearby. His dog often slept on this bridge. After the dog passed away, the artist made this statue in remembrance.

<u>Knocker and bell</u> (#205)
This is a nice example of how people would knock on the door in the old days, and now they use an electric bell.

Turn right into the *Agnietenstraat*.

<u>3 Stars</u>
<u>3 Ducks</u>
<u>3 Moons</u>
You can find them above every door on the right side. They are part of the coat of arms of the family who had these houses built for poor people. These are so called 'almshouses'. They are very small.

<u>2 Women</u> (Holding the building, left in the middle of the facade facing the *Lange Nieuwstraat*.)
You can also see keys, birds, flowers and more.

<u>Miffy</u> (In front of Miffy museum.)

Cafe Centraal. On the side of the Central Museum, serving food with Miffy images.

You will probably see a lot of cargo bikes. Dutch city parents use them to transport their small children. Continue straight ahead in the same street, now called *Nicolaaskerkhof* and then *Nicolaasstraat*. At the end you turn right into the *Twijnstraat*. Mind you, this is a normal street, so stay on the sidewalk. Cars usually drive carefully, bikes often don't.

Stael (#9). Lunchroom with kids' corner. In the back you can look out over the old canal.
(Many of the places lined up on the left side have window seats on the water side.)

Sector 3 (#7). Chocolate Miffys.

Walk on past the houses until you see the canal.

Bow and arrow (Across the water on the other side you can see a bow and arrow in a facade.)
These buildings used to belong to the arch brewery. The house in front, directly by the waterside, was the brewery itself.

Yellow bell (right side #386 bis, up on the facade)

Tea kettle (right side #374 right side in the facade right above street level)

Teapot on a tree trunk (It is by the water side on the wharf, below #366)

Hand holding a plant (right side #364 facade)

Three towers like the ones from a traditional chess board (Right side #344, on a blue background as part of a knight's guard, orange banner.)

On all street lanterns you can see a small red and white sign. This is the coat of arms of the city.

Unicorn (right side #338, facade)

Boat makers (right side #332 very high on the facade)

Boat at sea (right side #330)

Plaque showing a castle with a moat around it (right side #320)
You will see *Groot Payenborgh* and next to it *Klein Payenborg*. This means a big house and a small house. In the old days it was very costly to heat up the big houses, so they often built a smaller house next to it for winter. You can see this more often

along the canal.

Lion's head (to your left, on the bridge above the water)
This is the *Smeebrug*, referring to the smiths. Above the bridge you can see them at work. Left and right of the bridge are streets named after this trade and these streets lead to the city gate that was guarded by the smiths. The gate is no longer there, only a marking in the pavement.

Lion holding city armor (#304 right side, on the balcony on the corner)

There is a short while without any 'treasures'. There are some second hand stores though, which sometimes have funny stuff on display.

3 men carrying bags (right side #242)

Mermaid (right side #238)

The Joker, games store, (#230).

Princes en Erwtje, children's shoes and baby clothes, #220.

Turn left across the bridge (*Hamburgerbrug*) and go right past the canal.

Subcultures games, #183.

Cacao, chocolate store, expensive chocolate, also in Dom Tower shape, #179.

Stork (left side #171, very high up on the building)

You now enter the *Lijnmarkt*, a pedestrian zone.

Noahs, children's clothes, #45B.

Big glasses with one red glass and one blue glass (right side, #40)

Circular moon (left side #39A)

2 women (left side, #25, they are holding the facade)

It's a present, gift store, #16. A store where they have nothing you really need, but everything you want.

Left on the corner is **Bond & Smolders**, #16. One of the best pastries in town, selling Dom Tower cookies.

Knight on a horse (right side, #9)

Look left to the end of the street. In the distance, on a brown, brick building, you can see a UFO.

Turn right across the bridge. Often, in the good season, there is a pink ice caravan on the bridge. Walk over to the left side of the bridge and look out over the water. (Watch out for the traffic!)

Face (It is in the wall on the left side, underneath a lantern.)
It is the face of our King. He was born in Utrecht. He has 5 names, but his first name is *Willem-Alexander*.

Wooden shoes (Over the bridge on the right corner you can see wooden shoes and a bunch of other Dutch souvenirs.)

Continue in this *Servetstraat*. You will cross a metal plate in the ground. It marks the site of the old Roman wall from the 1st century when there was a small Roman fortress here, on the site of the Dom

Square. Sometimes there is steam coming from the

metal plate and at times it is lit.

On the right hand side, you will see a gate. Go inside and you will find a courtyard, quiet and green. In the far right corner is a display of Utrecht in its old days, next to the glass doors of a workshop. Peek inside: this is where they restore and repair the mechanical instruments that will be on display in the Museum of Self-playing Instruments.
In the wall leading towards the workshop, you can see 8 triangles. In the third from the left, marked #2, you will see Saint Martin. He is a saint who once shared half his coat with a poor man. He could only give half of it, because the other half belonged to the Roman emperor. His coat was red and his underwear white: this is why these two colours are the colours of Utrecht.

Black panther (on the wall above #5)

Go back through the gate. Straight ahead on the left side is Lebowski. Not designed for kids, but there is a lot to see, like a stuffed giraffe.

Possible games

Who can spot the first:

☺ Bike with only one wheel
☺ Bike with more than 2 locks
☺ Yellow & blue bike
☺ Pink Bicycle Bell
☺ Red Bicycle Bell

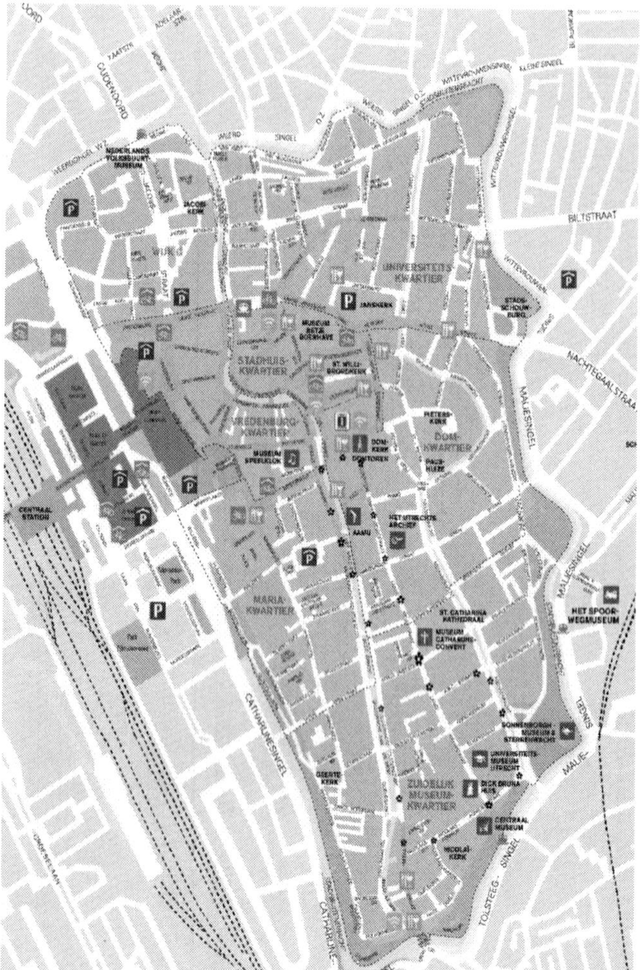
UNIVERSITEITS KWARTIER
STADHUIS-KWARTIER
VREDENBURG-KWARTIER
MARIA-KWARTIER
DOM-KWARTIER
ZUIDELIJK MUSEUM-KWARTIER
CENTRAAL STATION
HET SPOORWEGMUSEUM
BILTSTRAAT
NACHTEGAALSTRAAT
MALIESINGEL
CATHARIJNESINGEL
TOLSTEEG-SINGEL
VENUSLAAN
VONDELLAAN
JANSKERK
DOMKERK
DOMTOREN
PIETERSKERK
MUSEUM SPEELKLOK
ST. CATHARINA KATHEDRAAL
CENTRAAL MUSEUM
DICK BRUNA HUIS
NICOLAI-KERK
STADSSCHOUWBURG

9. Practical Information

School Vacations
There are several school vacations throughout the year. The country is divided into 3 regions, each having different vacation dates to spread the crowds. If you want to avoid the masses, check out when each vacation is:
2017: http://www.schoolvakanties-nederland.nl/schoolvakanties-2017.html
2018: https://www.schoolvakanties-nederland.nl/schoolvakanties-2018.html
Basisonderwijs - elementary school
Voortgezet onderwijs - high school
Utrecht is in the middle region – *midden*.

Some language in order to understand Dutch websites:

januari	–	January
februari	–	February
maart	–	March
april	–	April
mei	–	May
juni	–	June
juli	–	July

augustus	–	August
september	–	September
oktober	–	October
november	–	November
december	–	December
maandag	–	Monday
dinsdag	–	Tuesday
woensdag	–	Wednesday
donderdag	–	Thursday
vrijdag	–	Friday
zaterdag	–	Saturday
zondag	–	Sunday
open	–	open
gesloten	–	closed
openingstijden	–	opening hours

Also available:

Utrecht: Sights and Secrets of Holland's Smartest City. The travel guide for Utrecht.

Utrecht & Food
Let your taste buds lead you through Utrecht.

Peace & Porridge
A Dutch view of fake eggs, plastic cheese and of course Mahna Mahna.

Utrecht & Religion
For those fascinated by religion and history.

Utrecht & Water
Do you love water and boating? Plunge in.

Thank you for reading!
If you enjoyed the ride, please leave a review!

And follow us on Facebook (Secrets of Utrecht) and YouTube (Behind the Sights) for more about Utrecht, fun, facts, pictures and news about promotions and upcoming books.